D1505701

BATTLE OF
WATERLOO

BY JOHN HAMILTON

VISIT US AT
WWW.ABDOPUBLISHING.COM

Published by ABDO Publishing Company, PO Box 398166, Minneapolis, MN 55439. Copyright ©2014 by Abdo Consulting Group, Inc. International copyrights reserved in all countries. No part of this book may be reproduced in any form without written permission from the publisher. ABDO & Daughters™ is a trademark and logo of ABDO Publishing Company.

Printed in the United States of America, North Mankato, Minnesota.
112013
012014

 PRINTED ON RECYCLED PAPER

Editor: Sue Hamilton
Graphic Design: Sue Hamilton
Cover Design: Neil Klinepier
Cover Photo: Getty Images
Interior Images: Alamy-pgs 15, 16, 17, 19, 24, 26, 27 & 28; Corbis-pgs 8-9, 21 & 29; Getty Images-pgs 1, 7, 14, 20, 23; John Hamilton-pgs 6 & 18; Thinkstock-pgs 10, 22, 31 & background images; Wikimedia Commons-pg 4 by artist Leo von Klenze, pg 5 by artist Jacques-Louis David; pg 11 by artist François Gérard; pg 12 by artist Thomas Lawrence; pg 13-replica of artist Paul Ernst Gebauer; pg 25 by artist Henri Felix Emmanuel Phillippoteaux.

ABDO Booklinks

To learn more about Great Battles, visit ABDO Publishing Company online. Web sites about Great Battles are featured on our Booklinks pages. These links are routinely monitored and updated to provide the most current information available. Web site: www.abdopublishing.com

Library of Congress Control Number: 2013946977

Cataloging-in-Publication Data

Hamilton, John. 1959-
 Battle of Waterloo / John Hamilton.
  p. cm. -- (Great battles)
Includes index.
ISBN 978-1-62403-207-3
1. Waterloo, Battle of, Waterloo, Belgium, 1815--Juvenile literature. 2. Napoleonic Wars, 1800-1815--Campaigns--Belgium--Waterloo--Juvenile literature. 3. Napoleon I, Emperor of the French,1769-1821--Military leadership--Juvenile literature. I. Title.
940.2/742--dc23

2013946977

CONTENTS

THE RETURN OF
NAPOLEON

In 1814, the leaders of Europe thought they had solved a big problem. France had finally been defeated in battle, after nearly 23 years of constant warfare that had cost millions of lives. French Emperor Napoleon Bonaparte, idolized by many of his citizens but considered a tyrant by most of Europe, was banished to the Mediterranean island of Elba, where he couldn't cause any more trouble. But not for long.

On February 26, 1815, Napoleon escaped by boat from his island prison less than a year after being thrown from power. When he landed on French soil, he was hailed by many as a hero. By the time he made his way to the French capital of Paris in March,

Napoleon in exile on Elba.

he had amassed an army of almost 125,000 soldiers. The unpopular French King Louis XVIII was forced to flee. Napoleon had become the emperor of France once more. He had another chance to fulfill his ambition of creating a European empire ruled by France.

Several European countries immediately declared war on the outlaw Napoleon. The alliance was called the 7th Coalition (it was the seventh time countries had agreed to fight France in the previous quarter century). The European countries lined up to fight Napoleon this time included the United Kingdom, Austria, Prussia, Russia, Sweden, and the Netherlands.

A portrait of Napoleon Bonaparte leading his troops through the Great St. Bernard pass in the Swiss Alps.

PREPARATION FOR BATTLE

In early spring 1815, the Allied powers assembled their armies and began to march on France, intent on removing Napoleon from power. Their plan was to mass their troops on the French border, and then attack simultaneously, crushing the enemy and moving as quickly as possible toward Paris.

Field Marshal Arthur Wellesley, the Duke of Wellington, led the army of the United Kingdom, plus Allied forces from the Netherlands, Belgium, and German states. In total, he commanded about 67,000 soldiers. Prussian Marshal Gebhard von Blücher led more than 100,000 soldiers. Together, these two huge armies massed together in Belgium, on the northeast border of France. Because of the vast distances involved, and the lack of rail service, the armies of Russia and Austria would be delayed.

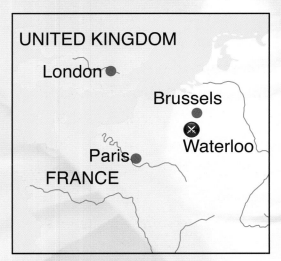

Napoleon's plan to divide the coalition forces

French
Prussian
British/Allies

*Borders are present day

A reenactment of Napoleon and his army on the battlefield at Waterloo.

Napoleon was the master of winning battles by attacking first. He decided to destroy the armies of Wellington and Blücher and capture the city of Brussels, in modern-day Belgium, before the other Allies could even arrive. After such a victory, he would have the upper hand and could negotiate a peace treaty that favored France.

Even though his army of about 100,000 men was outnumbered by almost two-to-one, Napoleon had a plan: he would drive his troops through the center of the Allied armies and separate them from each other. Then, he would destroy each enemy army in turn, first the Prussians, and then Wellington's forces.

Napoleon's army clashed with the enemy twice before the main battle, once at a crossroads called Quatre-Bra, and also at Ligny. The two sides fought to a stalemate at Quatre-Bra, but the Prussians were badly mauled at Ligny and were forced to withdraw, just as Napoleon had hoped. Wellington was surprised at the direction of the French attack. "Napoleon has humbugged me," he said.

Napoleon sent over 30,000 troops, under the command of Marshal Emmanuel de Grouchy, to pursue the Prussians and prevent them from linking up again with the British. Napoleon then prepared the remainder of his army, about 73,000 men, to attack Wellington and his collection of Allied forces.

Napoleon was mistaken in believing that the Prussians were destroyed. Despite the many dead or wounded at Ligny, they were able to retreat and regroup. They went north, not east as Napoleon supposed. If the French emperor had known just how close the large Prussian army was to his position, he might not have been so confident that he could crush Wellington.

The Duke of Wellington was a master of defensive tactics. In warfare, it is usually much more difficult to attack than it is to defend.

Wellington's army on the road to Quatre-Bra.

Wellington moved his army north to a spot he had scouted earlier. He lined his men up along a low ridge about two miles (3.2 km) long called Mont St. Jean. They were just south of a small village that would soon bear the name of one of the greatest battles ever fought—Waterloo.

LEADERS OF
FRANCE

Napoleon Bonaparte

Emperor **Napoleon Bonaparte** (1769-1821) led France from 1804 to 1815. As a politician and general, he rose to power during the French Revolution, which resulted in the execution of King Louis XVI.

Napoleon was born in Corsica in 1769. He went to military school, then became a brilliant commander in the French army. He was especially skilled at military organization and training. He could be moody and short-tempered, but he was one of the greatest military leaders in history. He gained almost fanatical respect and loyalty from his soldiers. His ambition seemed limitless. Napoleon entered politics in 1799 after helping overthrow the current revolutionary government, which was in crisis at the time.

During Napoleon's reign as emperor, he reformed the French legal and tax systems, fixed roads and sewers, established the Bank of France, and supported education. He also wanted to spread his ideas throughout Europe, creating a French empire with Paris at its center. He sent his armies across Europe, plunging the continent into almost continuous war for many years. At the height of his power, Napoleon's France had conquered much of Europe. The Napoleonic Wars resulted in an estimated three to six million deaths.

After a disastrous invasion of Russia in 1812, which left his army in tatters, Napoleon was forced to give up power in 1814. A coalition of other European countries banished the emperor to the Mediterranean island of Elba, west of Italy. During his almost year-long exile, Napoleon plotted his eventual escape, leading to his return as emperor and his final, fateful battle at Waterloo.

Michel Ney

Marshal Michel Ney (1769-1815) was one of France's top military leaders during the French Revolution and the Napoleonic Wars. Born to a working-class family in 1769, he enlisted in the French military in 1787 at age 18. As he rose through the ranks, he fought in many wars and was wounded several times. Napoleon once called Ney "the bravest of the brave." When Napoleon returned to France from his exile in Elba, Ney vowed to arrest him and bring him back alive in an iron cage. Instead, he joined Napoleon's growing army and helped the emperor's return to power. Ney commanded Napoleon's left wing at the Battle of Waterloo. He was criticized for acting too slowly and making critical battlefield errors. After Napoleon was defeated and dethroned by the European Allied armies, Ney was arrested and executed by firing squad.

LEADERS OF THE ALLIES

Arthur Wellesley, the Duke of Wellington (1769-1852) led one of the two major armies that fought against Napoleon's French forces at the Battle of Waterloo in 1815. Wellington commanded a mixed force of soldiers from the United Kingdom, the Netherlands, Belgium, and several German states.

Wellington was born in Dublin, Ireland, in 1769. He joined the army in 1787 at age 17. He soon proved his worth as a leader in India and in Europe fighting against France. He was known for his great preparation for battle, and for being a master of defensive fighting when necessary. Although he had a reputation for being aloof, he had a genuine concern for the well-being of his soldiers, which earned him much respect and loyalty.

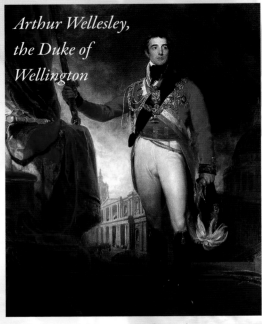

Arthur Wellesley, the Duke of Wellington

After a long period in the military, Wellington was knighted and became a member of the British Parliament. In 1808, he reentered the military, taking control of Allied forces aligned against France during the Peninsular War in Spain and Portugal. His major victory in this war earned him the title Duke of Wellington.

In 1818, three years after defeating Napoleon at Waterloo, Wellington returned to politics. In 1827, he became the commander in chief of the British army, and in 1828 became the prime minister of the United Kingdom.

Gebhard Leberecht von Blücher (1742-1819) was a Prussian field marshal who led his army, together with the Duke of Wellington's forces, against Napoleon

Gebhard von Blücher

at Waterloo in 1815. He had a reputation for being aggressive and direct, both in war and in his personal life. While he lacked imagination on the battlefield, his determination often resulted in victory.

Blücher was born in 1742 in present-day northern Germany. He joined the army at age 16. After nearly two decades spent as a cavalry soldier, Blücher retired and became a successful farmer. In 1787, he returned to military duty and fought against the French. In 1801, he was promoted to lieutenant general. He was so blunt and outspoken that he was almost dismissed several times, but he always kept his job because of his value as an aggressive army commander. In 1813, he was promoted to field marshal, the highest rank in the Prussian military.

At the time of the Battle of Waterloo in 1815, Blücher was 72 years old. During the clash at Ligny, just before Waterloo, he lay trapped under his dead horse for hours while cavalry rode over and around him. After being freed, he rejoined his army and led it to Waterloo by late afternoon, just in time to join Wellington's forces.

TACTICS AND
WEAPONS

Warfare of the early 1800s relied on three very different parts of the military: the massed attack of infantry (foot soldiers), the devastating power of artillery (cannons), and the quick-striking ability of cavalry (troops on horseback).

Infantry made up the bulk of each side's armies during the Battle of Waterloo. Soldiers were armed with the most common weapon of the time—the flintlock musket.

Muskets had smooth bores (the inside of the barrel), and were inaccurate when fired at targets a long distance away. To make up for this, soldiers stood in long lines, shoulder to shoulder, sometimes two or three rows deep. When ordered, they fired a volley of deadly lead balls all at once toward the enemy. After a row of soldiers fired, they stepped backward and a second row took their place, allowing the first row time to reload.

Actors with flintlock muskets and bayonets.

Actors dressed as British soldiers load their muskets to reenact the Battle of Waterloo.

The most common British musket was the Brown Bess. British soldiers also used Baker rifles, which were more accurate than muskets, but slower to load and fire. The standard French infantry weapon was the Charleville smoothbore musket. Most of the muskets and rifles of the time could be outfitted with bayonets for close-quarter fighting.

Besides keeping them warm, the infantry's colorful uniforms helped them tell friend from foe. Uniforms also had a psychological purpose.

Epaulets made the men's shoulders seem wider and thicker, giving a similar effect as padded shoulders in a suit of clothing made today. Also, helmets and bearskin hats were built tall. Together, the epaulets and tall hats made soldiers seem bigger and stronger than they really were. To an enemy soldier, especially one who might already be stunned by the horrors of war, witnessing a massed group of gigantic enemy troops rushing forward would be a terrifying sight indeed.

A single blast from a cannon could kill a dozen or more soldiers at once.

Cannons were the most deadly weapons on the battlefield. A single artillery blast could kill a dozen or more soldiers at once. It took several men working in unison to move, aim, load, and fire each artillery weapon, called a "piece." Early in Napoleon's military career, he trained as an artillery officer. He had a healthy respect for just how deadly cannons could be. French artillery forces were well trained and feared by every foe.

The most common artillery ammunition was a solid iron ball called round shot. It cut through troops with ease, severing arms and legs as it rolled and bounced across the ground at high speed. Canister shot was a cylinder filled with metal balls. When fired, it turned the cannon into a giant shotgun, scattering the balls into onrushing enemy soldiers. Its destructive power was frightful. During muddy conditions, such as those at the Battle of Waterloo, round shot was less effective. The heavy iron balls tended to plow into the soft ground and come to a stop. Also, the mud made it difficult for the horse-drawn carts on which the cannons were mounted to be moved around on the battlefield.

Cavalry troops were the elite fighting forces of armies in the early 1800s. Soldiers mounted on horseback were always a force to be reckoned with. Because horses are so swift, even a small cavalry unit could surprise and overpower a group of soldiers on foot. Attacking lines of enemy infantry from the sides or rear could be especially devastating. Cavalry charges during the Napoleonic Wars sometimes involved thousands of horses charging at once. Just the sight of these ground-shaking mass charges sent fear into even the most grizzled infantry veterans. When the cavalry charged into a group of foot soldiers, they slashed downward with their sabers. Many of the enemy were also trampled underfoot.

Cavalry charges were seldom performed alone. Full charges across an open field against prepared soldiers and cannons could be suicide. To help their horsemen, armies usually first fired artillery into the enemy to wound as many as possible and scatter them. Infantry on the flanks would also fire into the enemy to further "soften" them before the cavalry reached its destination.

The best way to stop a cavalry attack was with another group of cavalry. Opposing groups of horsemen could often be seen swirling around in mortal combat on the edges of the battlefield. In addition to attacking the enemy, cavalry was also valuable in quickly scouting the enemy's location, as well as attacking supply lines, such as wagons carrying food or ammunition.

THE FIRST FRENCH
ATTACK

At dawn on the morning of June 18, 1815, soldiers of both Napoleon and Wellington's armies awoke. They were wet and miserable, having endured a night of torrential rain. Both commanders assessed their positions.

Wellington's forces were lined up at Mont St. Jean, a low ridge about two miles (3.2 km) long, stretching east to west. Below them was a shallow valley with gentle slopes. About a mile (1.6 km) to the south was another low ridge. This was where Napoleon lined up his French forces facing the Allies. The two armies were about evenly matched in numbers, but Napoleon's forces had many battle-hardened veterans, plus superior artillery and cavalry.

Napoleon decided not to attack right away. Because of the overnight rains, the ground was muddy. This made it much more difficult to move heavy artillery around on the battlefield.

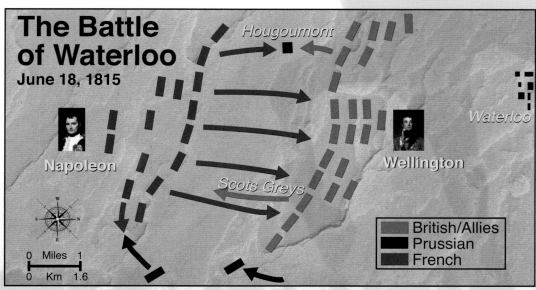

The Battle of Waterloo
June 18, 1815

Hougoumont

Napoleon

Scots Greys

Wellington

Waterloo

0 Miles 1
0 Km 1.6

British/Allies
Prussian
French

Also, the fired cannonballs would mostly plop into the mud instead of rolling and injuring the enemy troops. Napoleon wanted time for the ground to dry out as much as possible. Little did the emperor know, however, that Prussian troops led by Marshal Blücher were on their way to reinforce Wellington. Napoleon's delay meant that the Prussians would play a fateful role in the battle later that day.

Many French officers were worried about opposing Wellington. They remembered previous British victories in Spain and Portugal. Napoleon scoffed and said, "I tell you that Wellington is a bad general, that the English are bad troops, and that this will be a picnic."

A reenactment of Napoleon addressing his troops.

British troops defend the farmhouse Hougoumont against a French attack during the Battle of Waterloo.

Napoleon wanted to attack Wellington's center. But first, he launched a diversion. At 11:30 a.m., he sent a large force to attack a farmhouse with high walls that was occupied by British forces. Called Hougoumont, it was situated on the far western side of the battlefield. Napoleon hoped Wellington would send extra troops to the besieged chateau and weaken his center. Wellington never took the bait, sending only the minimum troops needed to defend Hougoumont, which luckily never fell to the French.

Finally, at about 1:00 p.m., a group of 80 French cannons began firing on Wellington's center line on the hill. This frightful artillery barrage, which lasted about 30 minutes, was meant to "soften up" the enemy to make it easier for Napoleon's infantry troops. Wellington, seeing how vulnerable his soldiers were to the withering French artillery attack, ordered the men to move to the far side of the ridge, where the ground would partially deflect the cannonballs. He also urged them to lie down, which made them less of a target. Even with these precautions, many Allied troops were torn apart by the French bombardment.

Napoleon next ordered an infantry attack of the enemy's center. Four divisions of men, about 18,000 French soldiers under the command of Marshal Jean-Baptise Drouet, Comte d'Erlon, moved across the valley in several long columns, shoulder to shoulder. Then, to the march of French war drums, they moved up the ridge in lockstep. Marshal d'Erlon's men suffered terribly under the barrage of Wellington's artillery at the top of the hill. The slaughter was frightful. As the enemy drew near, Wellington ordered his men to stand and advance to the exposed side of the ridge and prepare to meet the attackers.

When the French reached the top of the ridge, their superior numbers and experience seemed to turn the tide. They fired volley after volley of musket shot into the enemy's ranks. Several British units were smashed. A Belgian unit, its morale shattered, broke and ran away. Marshal d'Erlon's troops had a chance now to split Wellington's army in two.

The French artillery firing cannons at British troops.

The charge of the Royal Scots Greys.

Before the French could take advantage of this gap in the line, British troops under the command of General Sir Thomas Picton poured in and held off the French assault, although Picton was killed. The fighting grew desperate as the French bravely pressed on and tried to keep their hold on the ridge. The two sides fought savagely at close quarters with muskets and bayonets. The bodies of hundreds of dead and wounded soldiers littered the ground, and smoke filled the air.

The infantry was in desperate need of help. At this point, Wellington ordered two cavalry brigades to counter-attack. Nearly 2,000 horses and their mounts thundered over the ridge. The cavalry charged downhill and crashed into the mass of French soldiers, slashing their way through the infantry with their swords and sabers. Part of this group was the Royal Scots Greys cavalry regiment. As they passed by foot soldiers of the 92nd Regiment of Scottish Highlanders, the troops shouted "Scotland forever!"

The Scots Greys and other cavalry units galloped forward, continuing their charge even as the French infantry scattered and ran.

Gripped in a sort of battle fever and ignoring calls to fall back, the cavalry charged across the valley directly into the French artillery lines. They slashed at the gun crews and put many of the cannons out of action. But now they were in the midst of Napoleon's army, with their horses exhausted and no reserves to protect them. The French surrounded the British cavalry and cut them to ribbons. Only a small percentage escaped the brutal French counterattack.

Marshal d'Erlon's infantry attack on Wellington's center had cost the French dearly, with thousands dead or wounded, and nearly 3,000 French soldiers taken prisoner. But the Allied forces had suffered greatly also.

Meanwhile, Napoleon discovered an ominous new threat: Prussian troops had been sighted to the east. It was an advance unit of Marshal Blücher's army, arriving at Waterloo at last to help Wellington.

Because of the Prussians, Napoleon was forced to send precious reserve troops and ammunition to his right flank. It was already mid-afternoon. The emperor could hold off the new threat temporarily, but the full Prussian army would soon arrive. Napoleon was running out of time.

Napoleon questions a captured Prussian soldier.

MARSHAL NEY'S CAVALRY
CHARGE

After surviving French Marshal d'Erlon's disastrous frontal attack, Wellington regrouped and shuffled his reserve forces, shoring up his battle lines to defend against another assault. As both sides again began trading artillery fire, Wellington once more withdrew his men behind the ridge for protection, where they were out of sight. He also began evacuating hundreds of wounded soldiers away from the battlefield.

On the opposite ridge, at about 3:00 p.m., French Marshal Ney observed the enemy with his field glasses. Through the smoky haze, he watched as the British wounded were evacuated down the road that led to the city of Brussels. Ney mistakenly believed Wellington's entire army was retreating. He ordered his cavalry to hunt the enemy down. Marshal Ney would personally lead the charge.

Marshal Ney leads the French cavalry charge against Wellington's forces.

British soldiers form "infantry squares" to defend against the French cavalry.

More than 5,000 French cavalry troops swept up the ridge toward the enemy. The French artillery went silent so they wouldn't hit their own cavalry. To the British and Allied forces watching from their stations, it was a fearsome sight. The ground literally shook as the French charged forward.

Wellington quickly ordered his men to form 20 large "infantry squares" behind the ridge. On each side of a square, a row of kneeling men firmly held their bayonets up and outward. Horses refused to charge into such a wall of glinting steel. Behind the kneeling troops were two more ranks of soldiers armed with muskets. Artillery was lined up in front of the squares.

As the French cavalry came up the hill, they were met with murderous rounds of cannon fire. The artillery crews then fled to the interior of the squares. As the French cavalry swirled around the squares in frustration, they were picked off by musket fire.

Time after time, the French cavalry charged and were repelled. Marshal Ney had four horses shot out from under him. Finally, Ney and the surviving cavalry troops gave up and retreated back to the French line.

ATTACK OF THE
IMPERIAL GUARD

As the day turned to early evening, Napoleon grew increasingly frustrated. Marshal Blücher's Prussian forces were threatening to break through on Napoleon's right side. Many of the emperor's reserve troops were now fighting a grim battle with the Prussians instead of attacking Wellington. The Allied forces had survived the massive French cavalry attack, but Wellington's line was

A member of Napoleon's Imperial Guard.

badly mauled and in danger of collapsing. Napoleon sensed that he had one last chance at victory.

At 7:00 p.m., Napoleon sent about 3,000 of his elite Imperial Guard soldiers to make another frontal attack against Wellington's center. These battle-hardened veterans were the last of the French reserves. They had never before lost in battle. If they did not succeed this time, all would be lost.

As the day ended, Wellington's forces overwhelmed the French Imperial Guard. Napoleon and his soldiers were forced to flee the battlefield.

The proud Imperial Guard marched in formation up the ridge. The British were waiting for them. Once the Guard reached the top of the hill, the British rose up and fired their muskets at point-blank range. The Guard fought back valiantly, but they faced overwhelming odds. British reserve troops and cavalry added to the carnage. Finally, the Guard broke and began fleeing down the hill.

Wellington waved his hat in the air and urged his men to pursue the enemy.

Panic gripped the French soldiers. The unthinkable had happened: the Imperial Guard were actually retreating! The retreat turned into a chaotic rout. Anguished cries of "Every man for himself!" echoed across the battlefield.

In the gathering dusk, the French fled the battlefield. Napoleon's royal carriage became stuck in the mud, and he was forced to flee on his white horse. For Napoleon, after a day filled with carnage and lost hope, the Battle of Waterloo was over.

THE BATTLE'S
AFTERMATH

The Battle of Waterloo broke the back of Napoleon's invasion force. Across the battlefield lay at least 25,000 dead or wounded French soldiers. Another 8,000 were taken prisoner. The Allies lost a combined 22,000 casualties. (During the entire June campaign, more than 70,000 men on both sides were killed or wounded.) For several days afterwards, many of the wounded lingered on the blood-soaked battlefield before they were sent to hospitals. Many others died of their wounds.

After the battle, Napoleon fled home to Paris, France, pursued by the Allies. He was forced to surrender to the British on July 15, 1815. A peace treaty restored King Louis XVIII to the French throne.

The Battle of Waterloo broke Napoleon's invasion force. Defeated, the emperor fled back to Paris. He was arrested nearly a month later on July 15, 1815.

Napoleon was banished to the desolate island of Saint Helena on October 16, 1815.

Although he hoped to regain power, he never left his island exile. He died on May 5, 1821.

Waterloo was the Duke of Wellington's last battle. He led the Allied occupation of France, and urged that the French people be treated leniently, and with fairness. Wellington became the prime minister of the United Kingdom in 1828.

The British eventually banished Napoleon to the island of Saint Helena, in the middle of the Atlantic Ocean. He lived in exile for six years, dying in May 1821, possibly of stomach cancer, at the age of 51.

The Battle of Waterloo capped what historians now call the "Hundred Days" (the period between Napoleon's return from exile on Elba and King Louis XVIII returning to power—actually 111 days). It marked the end of Napoleon's remarkable story. It also signaled, thanks to the cooperation of the Allied countries, the beginning of nearly 100 years of relative peace and prosperity for Europe.

GLOSSARY

ARTILLERY

Large weapons of war, such as cannons, mortars, and howitzers, that are used by military forces on land and at sea to hurl projectiles such as cannonballs at the enemy.

CAVALRY

During the Napoleonic era, soldiers who rode and fought on horseback were called cavalry. Modern cavalry includes soldiers who fight in armored vehicles such as tanks or attack helicopters.

FLINTLOCK

A weapon such as a musket, rifle, or pistol, which is fired using the flintlock system created in the early 1600s. When the firearm's trigger is pulled, a hammer with a flint tip strikes a metal plate, causing a spark. This spark ignites the gunpowder inside the barrel. The resulting explosion forces the lead ball-shaped bullet out of the barrel.

FRENCH REVOLUTION

An uprising of common people in France against King Louis XVI and other members of royalty. The Revolution lasted from 1789 to 1799. It was a reaction to Louis XVI's corrupt government, spurred on by economic hardship among the lower classes of people. In 1792, Louis XVI was executed. Although the Revolution changed French society (and later much of the world), the radicals in charge were never able to form a stable government. Napoleon Bonaparte took power as dictator in 1799, and as emperor in 1804.

Napoleon Bonaparte

NAPOLEONIC WARS

A long series of wars between the armies of Napoleon and several coalition countries that banded together to fight the French Empire. The Napoleonic Wars lasted from about 1803 to 1815, and cost millions of lives.

PRUSSIA

A former German kingdom. At its peak, its borders covered most of present-day northeastern Germany and Poland. Prussia was well-known for its powerful and efficient military forces.

SABER

A sword with a curved, single edge. They were often used by cavalry troops as slashing weapons against ground infantry.

SMOOTHBORE

Smoothbore weapons are constructed with barrels—the part the bullet travels down—that are smooth on the inside. When the weapon is fired, the loose-fitting ammunition bounces from side to side until it emerges from the barrel. The bullet's motion greatly decreases the weapon's accuracy.

INDEX